FIRST ENGLISH SPELLING

FOR LEARNERS

Y H Mew
Anne Seaton

Illustrated by
Tan Choon Wai
Wong Swee Fatt

LEARNERS PUBLISHING

© 2001 Learners Publishing Pte Ltd

First published 2001 by
Learners Publishing Pte Ltd
25 Tagore Lane
#03-07 Singapore Godown
Singapore 787602

Email: learnpub@learners.com.sg
Website: http://www.learners.com.sg

ISBN 981 4070 28 9

Printed by Press Ace Pte Ltd, Singapore

To Teachers and Parents

English spelling must be mastered for the full understanding of word formation in English, and for vocabulary development. Good spelling is one of the key elements of good writing.

First English Spelling for Learners has been specially written for young learners. It introduces the basic rules of spelling, covering letter sounds, noun endings such as *-s, -es, -er, -or*; verb endings such as *-s, -es, -ing, -d, -ed*; adjective endings such as *-ful* and *-less*; and the adverb ending *-ly*. Much attention has been paid to the presentation and layout of this book in order to make it learner-friendly.

It is hoped not only that this book will give young learners a clear idea of the basic rules of spelling, but also that they will get a lot of enjoyment from the varied vocabulary specially chosen for their age group.

What you'll find in this book

1 The Alphabet and Letter Sounds

An **alphabet** is a set of **letters** that you use to make words. In the English alphabet there are **26 letters**, all with their own sounds. These 26 letters are arranged in a fixed order, called **alphabetical order**, or **ABC order**. You can write the letters in two forms: **small letters** or **capital letters**.

Small Letters

The **small letters** are also called **lower-case letters**. This is the way you write the small letters.

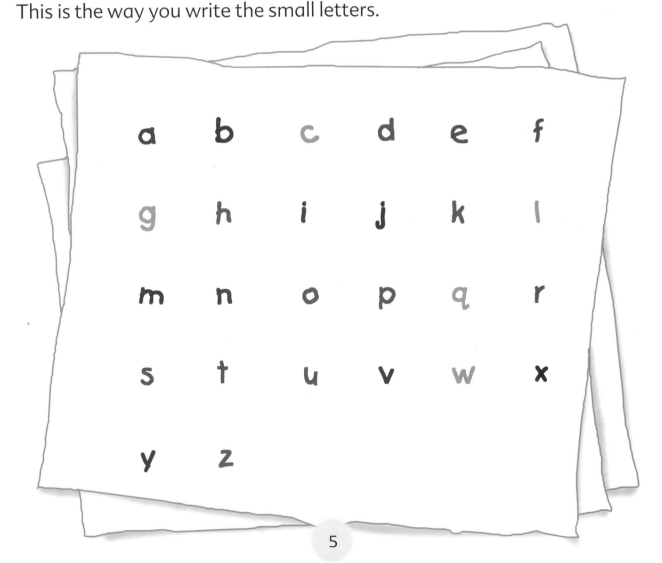

Capital Letters

Capital letters are also called **big letters**, or **upper-case letters**. This is the way you write the capital letters.

A B C D E
F G H I J
K L M N O
P Q R S T
U V
W X
Y Z

Did You Know

You use a capital letter for
▸ **the first letter in a sentence:** *The dog is barking.*
▸ **the word I:** *Tom and I are playing chess.*
▸ **names of people:** *Peter, John, Ali, Mary, Snow White.*
▸ **names of places:** *Paris, Botanic Gardens, Hyde Park, the Arctic.*
▸ **names of mountains and rivers:** *Mount Fuji, the Yellow River.*
▸ **the days of the week:** *Monday, Tuesday, Wednesday.*
▸ **the months of the year:** *January, February, March.*

Vowels

The English alphabet has two kinds of letters: **vowels** and **consonants.**

There are five vowels:

Look at these words. All of them have a vowel in the middle.

cat	rat	mat
bed	net	hen
bin	pin	fin
log	dot	fox
mug	hug	cup

Did You Know

There are two very short words that are made up of a single vowel:

I   a

Short Vowels

Some vowels have a short quick sound.

In these words, the vowels are short. Read them out aloud.

a	hand	bat	man	van
e	bell	hen	nest	pen
i	fish	fist	hill	milk
o	box	cot	dog	pond
u	duck	mud	nut	sun

Did You Know

The vowel **-u-** has a different short sound in these words. Read them out aloud.

bull	bush
cushion	full
pudding	pull
pussy	put

In some words, the letter **y** sounds like the short letter **i**. For example:

carry	city	easy
forty	lazy	party
silly	story	
baby	teddy	

You can put two vowels together to make a sound.

oo The pair of vowels **oo** can make a short sound like the *u* in **full**, **bull**, **bush** and **put**. Here are some words with the short *oo* sound in them.

cook	foot
good	hood
look	stood
wood	wool

ou The pair of vowels **ou** can also make the same short sound as this *u* and *oo*. Here are some words with the short *ou* sound in them.

could   should   would

ea The pair of vowels **ea** can make the same sound as the short vowel *e*. Here are some words with the short *ea* sound in them.

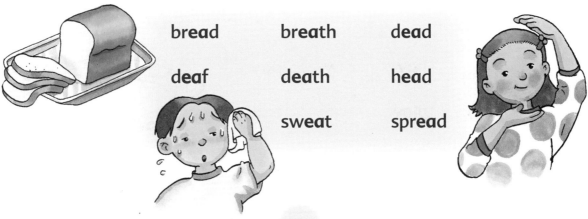

bread	breath	dead
deaf	death	head
	sweat	spread

Long Vowels

Some vowels have a long slow sound.

Long vowel _a_

cave	cage	cake	gate
face	lake	mane	spade

The pair of vowels **ai** has the same long _a_ sound.

rain	mail	rail
sail	train	pail

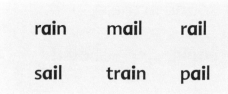

The pair of letters **ay** has the same long _a_ sound.

hay	day	pay
play	stay	tray

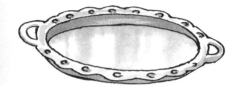

10

Long vowel *e*

The vowel **e** is long in these words.

eve   scene   these

The pair of vowels **ee** has the same long **e** sound.

jeep	**bee**f	**fee**t
peel	**see**	**shee**p
tree	**bee**	

The pair of vowels **ea** has the same long **e** sound in these words.

eat	**bea**d	**mea**l	**tea**m
meat	**lea**f	**sea**t	**sea**l

Long vowel *i*

The vowel **i** in these words is long.

nine	mice	ride
mile	kite	dive
tile	slide	wipe

The pair of vowels **ie** in these words has the same long *i* sound.

tie   lie   die   pie

The letter **y** in these words has the same long *i* sound.

fly	buy	dry
shy	sky	sly
spy	try	cry

Long vowel _o_

The vowel **o** in these words is long.

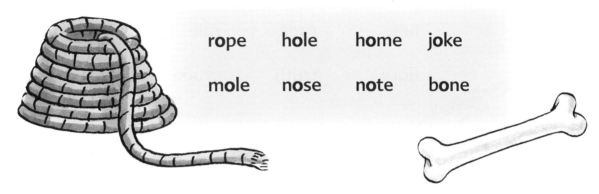

rope	hole	home	joke
mole	nose	note	bone

The pair of vowels **oa** in these words has the same long _o_ sound.

boat	coat	coal
foal	goal	goat
toad	road	

The pair of letters **ow** in these words has the same long _o_ sound.

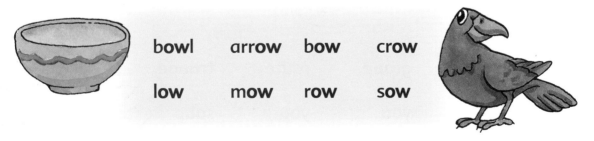

bowl	arrow	bow	crow
low	mow	row	sow

Long vowel *u*

The vowel **u** in these words is long.

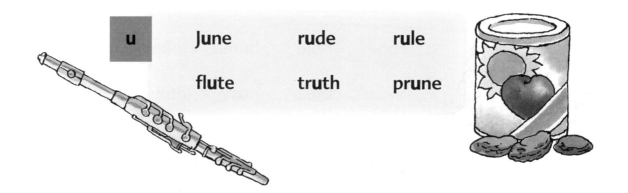

u	June	rude	rule
	flute	truth	prune

The pairs of letters **oo**, **ew**, **ue**, **ou** in these words have the same long *u* sound.

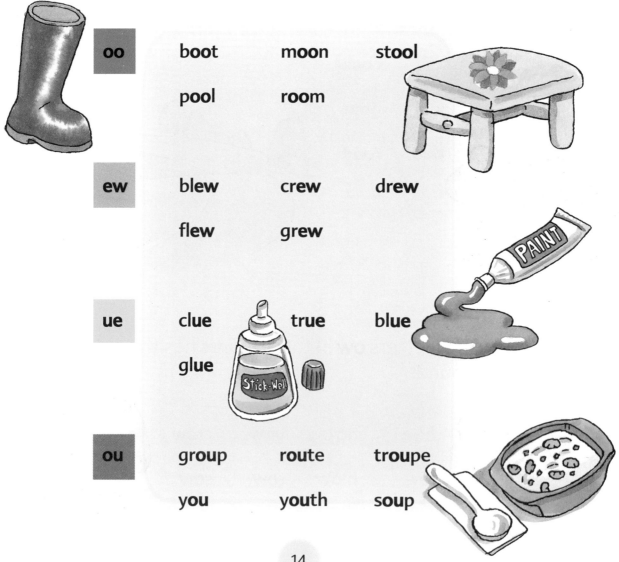

oo	boot	moon	stool
	pool	room	
ew	blew	crew	drew
	flew	grew	
ue	clue	true	blue
	glue		
ou	group	route	troupe
	you	youth	soup

Often **u**, **ew** and **ue** words have a *y* sound before them.

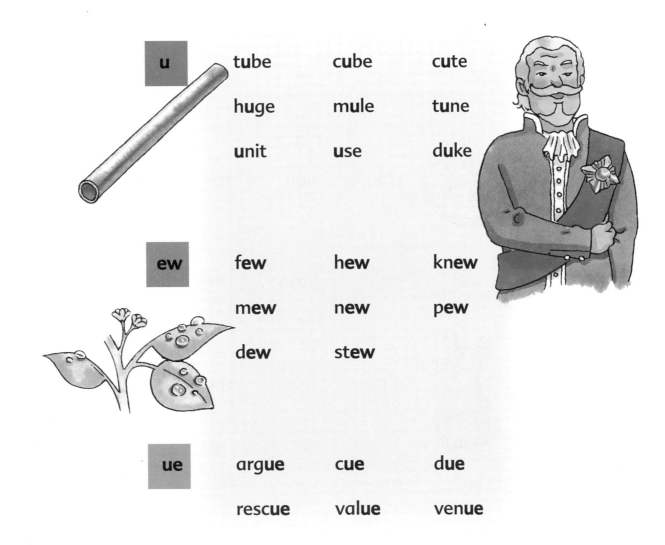

u	tube	cube	cute
	huge	mule	tune
	unit	use	duke
ew	few	hew	knew
	mew	new	pew
	dew	stew	
ue	argue	cue	due
	rescue	value	venue

These are some other long vowel sounds.

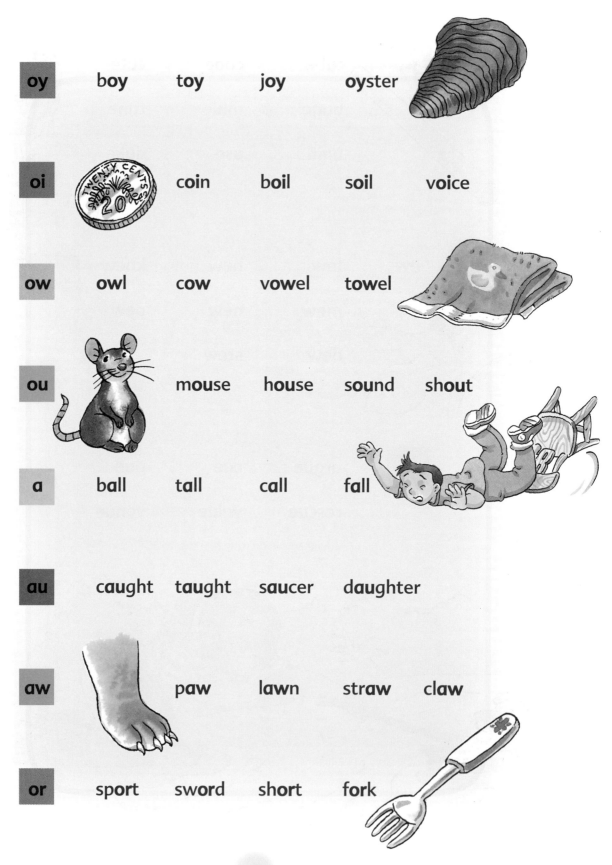

oy	boy	toy	joy	**oy**ster
oi		c**oi**n	b**oi**l	s**oi**l	v**oi**ce
ow	**ow**l	c**ow**	v**ow**el	t**ow**el
ou		m**ou**se	h**ou**se	s**ou**nd	sh**ou**t
a	b**a**ll	t**a**ll	c**a**ll	f**a**ll
au	c**au**ght	t**au**ght	s**au**cer	d**au**ghter
aw		p**aw**	l**aw**n	str**aw**	cl**aw**
or	sp**or**t	sw**or**d	sh**or**t	f**or**k

oa	roar	broad	board	oar
ou	bought	brought	sought	
a	plant	dance	chance	grass
ar	bark	farm	card	hard
al	half	calf	palm	calm
er	herd	term	serve	fern
ir	shirt	bird	girl	birthday
or	word	work	world	worm
ur	curl	burn	hurt	turn

Consonants

The other letters in the alphabet are called **consonants**.
They are:

b c d f g h j

k l m n p q r

s t v w x y z

Here are some words beginning with consonants.

bear   kite   scarf

car   lamb   turkey

deer   monkey   van

fox   nurse   wolf

goose   panda   xylophone

hare   queen   yak

jam   ring   zebra

Here are some pairs of consonants with special sounds.

sh

shark	**sh**eep	**sh**ell
shirt	**sh**ip	**sh**op
shadow	**sh**ort	cu**sh**ion

th

thin	**th**orn	**th**under
thick	**th**is	**th**at
thumb	**th**ese	**th**ose

ph

ele**ph**ant	tele**ph**one
photo	gra**ph**

Did You Know

The pair of consonants **ph** has the same sound as **f**.

The consonant **c** sounds the same as **k** when it comes before **a**, or **o**, or **u**.

calendar

cabin

camera

cobweb

cage

Word File

cab	**c**oin
cabbage	**c**old
cake	**c**ollar
calf	**c**olour
camp	**c**olt
canal	**c**omb
canoe	**c**omic
cap	**c**omputer
car	**c**ook
cat	**c**ow
cave	**c**ut
cobra	**c**ute
cock	**c**utlery

coffee

cuttlefish

20

The consonant **c** sounds like a **k** also when it comes before another consonant.

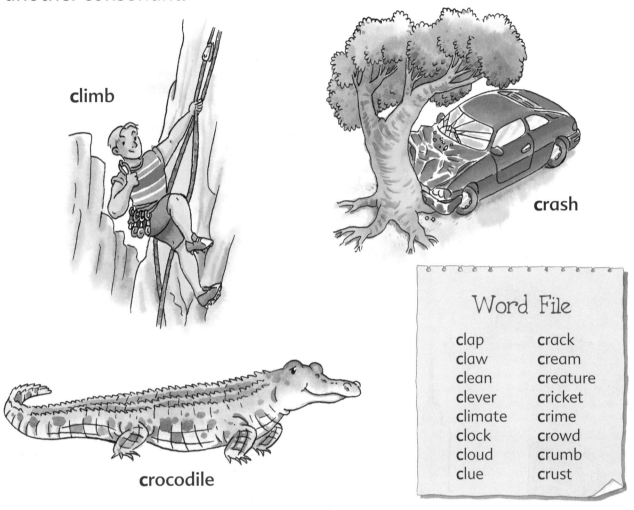

climb

crash

crocodile

Word File

clap	crack
claw	cream
clean	creature
clever	cricket
climate	crime
clock	crowd
cloud	crumb
clue	crust

The consonant **c** also sounds like a **k** at the end of a word.

CITY CLINIC

clinic

picnic

The consonant c sounds like s when it comes before e, or i, or y.

ceiling

circus

cereal

city

cyclist

Word File

celery   circle
cell   cycle
cent   cyclone
centre   cygnet
cigar   cylinder
cinema   cymbals

The double consonant **ch** often gives you a **k** sound.

chemist

choir

Word File

character
chorus
me**ch**anic
monar**ch**
stoma**ch**

Christmas

chrysanthemum

The double consonant **ch** also gives you a special sound
in these words.

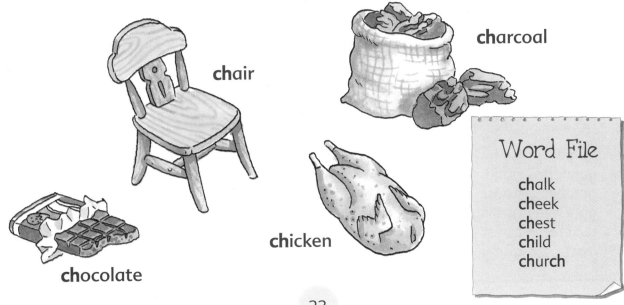

chair

charcoal

chicken

chocolate

Word File

chalk
cheek
chest
child
church

The consonant **g** has a hard **g** sound when it comes before **a**, or **o**, or **u**.

garlic

guava

goggles

gorilla

guppy

guitar

gondola

Word File

game	**g**olf
gander	**g**ood
garden	**g**oose
gate	**g**osling
gazelle	**g**uest
gold	**g**un

The consonant **g** has also a hard sound when it comes before another consonant.

globe

graph

gloves

grapes

grandfather

grandson

Word File

glad
gloomy
glue
grammar
grass
great
green

The consonant **g** also has a hard sound when it comes at the end of a word.

bug

bag

Word File

beg	Meg
big	dig
dog	fog
mug	hug
clog	slog

The consonant **g** usually has a soft sound when it comes before **e**, or **i**, or **y**.

gym

gypsy

gem

ginger

giant

giraffe

Did You Know

But there are lots of words in which **g** has a hard sound before **e** and **i**. Here are some examples:

gear   **g**ift
geese   **g**irl
get   **g**ive

Word File

gender
general
genius
geography

2 Syllables

A syllable is a part of a spoken word that you say as one sound. It usually has a vowel in it.

Some words have only **one** syllable. Here are some examples.

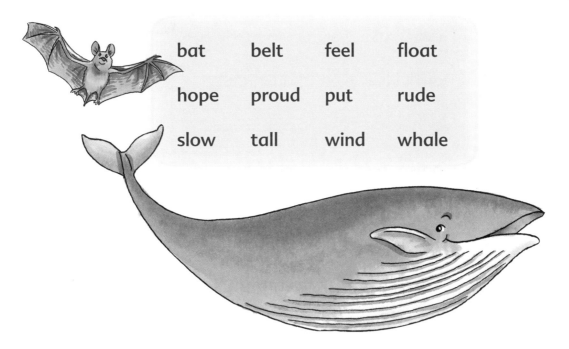

bat	belt	feel	float
hope	proud	put	rude
slow	tall	wind	whale

Some words have **two** syllables. Here are some examples.

clever	clev-er
common	com-mon
letter	let-ter
narrow	nar-row
polite	po-lite
quiet	qui-et
simple	sim-ple
stupid	stu-pid

Did You Know

If you can divide words into syllables it will help you in your spelling.

Some words have **three** syllables.

beautiful	beau-ti-ful
expensive	ex-pen-sive
capable	ca-pa-ble
confident	con-fi-dent
delicious	de-li-cious
difficult	dif-fi-cult
generous	gen-e-rous
poisonous	poi-son-ous
powerful	pow-er-ful

Some big words have **four** or **more** syllables.

comfortable	com-for-ta-ble
disappointed	dis-ap-point-ed
imaginative	i-ma-gi-na-tive
intelligent	in-tel-li-gent
interesting	in-te-res-ting
reasonable	rea-son-a-ble
valuable	val-u-a-ble

3 Some Basic Spelling Rules

You can add the **silent e** to some one-syllable words with short vowels to make new words with long vowels.

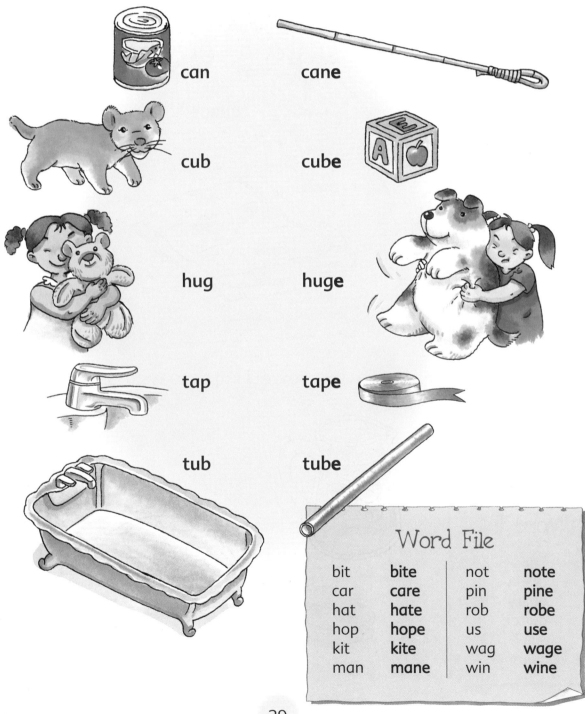

can	can**e**
cub	cub**e**
hug	hug**e**
tap	tap**e**
tub	tub**e**

Word File

bit	**bite**	not	**note**
car	**care**	pin	**pine**
hat	**hate**	rob	**robe**
hop	**hope**	us	**use**
kit	**kite**	wag	**wage**
man	**mane**	win	**wine**

The letter **q** is always followed by **u.**

quill

quack

queue

quilt

quarter

Word File

quarrel
queen
question
quick
quiet
quite
quiz

The vowel **u** comes before the vowel **i** in these words.

j**ui**ce

Word File

b**ui**ld
g**ui**de
g**ui**lty
g**ui**tar
s**ui**t
s**ui**table

fr**ui**t

The consonants **c** and **k** often go together at the end of
a one-syllable word containing a short vowel.

clock

truck

lock

track

knock

suck

kick

Word File

ba**ck**	flo**ck**
bla**ck**	lu**ck**
che**ck**	ne**ck**
chi**ck**	pe**ck**
co**ck**	plu**ck**
cra**ck**	sho**ck**
de**ck**	sti**ck**
du**ck**	ti**ck**

The consonant **k** is often followed by **e** or **i**.

kerb

kennel

ketchup

kitchen

king

kettle

kitten

kiwi

Word File

keep
keyboard
kid
kind
kindergarten
kiosk
kiss

The consonant l is often doubled at the end of one-syllable words.

hill

wall

well

yell

drill

bell

pull

Word File

ball	gill
bill	hall
bull	mill
call	roll
doll	sell
dull	tall
fall	tell
full	will

The consonant **s** is often doubled at the end of one-syllable words.

chess

mess

kiss

cross

press

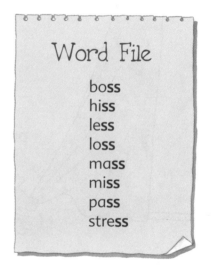

Word File

bo**ss**
hi**ss**
le**ss**
lo**ss**
ma**ss**
mi**ss**
pa**ss**
stre**ss**

The consonants **f** and **z** are often doubled at the end of one-syllable words.

buzzzz

buzz

cliff

puff

cuff

sniff

Word File

bluff	off
fizz	staff
huff	stiff
jazz	whizz

You often find a **silent e** after **s** or **z** at the end of a word.

chee**se**

ho**se**

snee**ze**

blou**se**

hou**se**

bree**ze**

Word File

bla**ze**	no**se**
clo**se**	prai**se**
da**ze**	pri**ze**
free**ze**	ro**se**
goo**se**	si**ze**
ha**ze**	va**se**
hor**se**	wi**se**

In some foreign words used in English, the consonant **k** often comes before **a** or **o**.

karate

kangaroo

kampung

koala

Word File

karaoke
kayak
kookaburra
Koran
kowtow

ie or *ei*?

When the sound is **ee**, **i** comes before **e**.

shield

Did You Know

But after the consonant **c**, **e** comes before **i**. For example:

cei ling
de cei ve
re cei ve

field

Word File

achieve
believe
brief
chief
niece
piece
priest
siege
yield

thief

The double vowel **ei** can also sound like the *ie* in **pie**.
Here are some examples:

either   h**ei**ght   n**ei**ther

The **ei** can sound like the *ay* in **way**. Here are some examples:

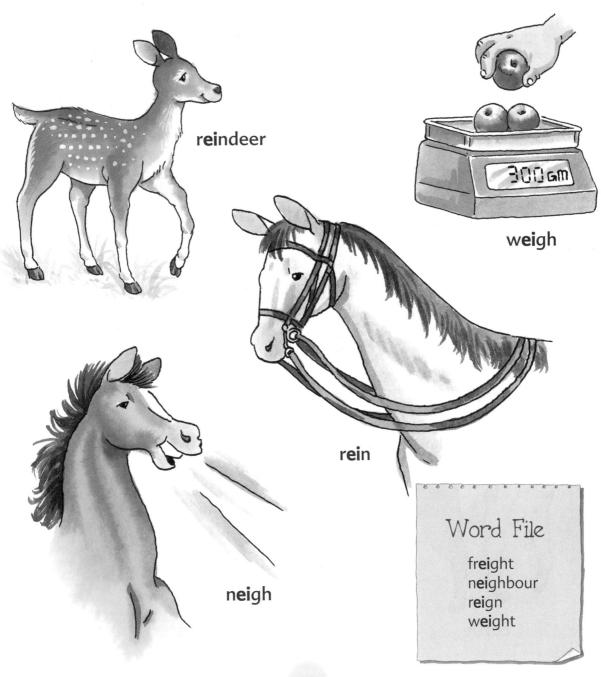

r**ei**ndeer

w**ei**gh

r**ei**n

n**ei**gh

Word File

fr**ei**ght
n**ei**ghbour
r**ei**gn
w**ei**ght

39

Short vowel words that end in **-le** have
a double consonant before **-le**.

apple

bottle

wa**ffle**

bubble

sa**ddle**

pu**ddle**

c**a**ttle

Word File

gi**gg**le
ke**tt**le
li**tt**le
mi**dd**le
pu**zz**le

After a long vowel, or a double vowel, there is only
one consonant before **-le**.

dou**ble**

noo**dle**

bee**tle**

cra**dle**

ta**ble**

ea**gle**

cy**cle**

Word File

ca**ble**
horri**ble**
nee**dle**
peo**ple**
ri**fle**
sta**ble**

4 Spelling Rules for Nouns

From Singular to Plural

When you are talking about two or more people, animals, places or things, you have to make the singular count nouns plural.

You add **-s** to most singular count nouns to make them plural.

dragon	+	**s**	=	dragons
carpet	+	**s**	=	carpets
cup	+	**s**	=	cups
dancer	+	**s**	=	dancers
egg	+	**s**	=	eggs
leopard	+	**s**	=	leopards
school	+	**s**	=	schools
shop	+	**s**	=	shops
window	+	**s**	=	windows

Word File

bag	**bags**
bank	**banks**
computer	**computers**
dog	**dogs**
door	**doors**
drawing	**drawings**
floor	**floors**
pen	**pens**
umbrella	**umbrellas**

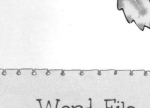

42

If the singular count nouns end in **-e**, you just add **-s** to make them plural.

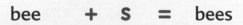

bee	+ **s**	=	bees
bike	+ **s**	=	bikes
cake	+ **s**	=	cakes
game	+ **s**	=	games
gate	+ **s**	=	gates
joke	+ **s**	=	jokes
kite	+ **s**	=	kites
plate	+ **s**	=	plates
spade	+ **s**	=	spades
whale	+ **s**	=	whales

Word File

cave	**caves**
circle	**circles**
date	**dates**
eye	**eyes**
game	**games**
note	**notes**
saddle	**saddles**
temple	**temples**

If the singular count nouns end in **-ge**, you just add **-s** to make them plural.

bridge	+	s =	bridges
badge	+	s =	badges
cage	+	s =	cages
edge	+	s =	edges
fridge	+	s =	fridges
hedge	+	s =	hedges
judge	+	s =	judges
page	+	s =	pages
ridge	+	s =	ridges
sponge	+	s =	sponges
stage	+	s =	stages

Did You Know

After adding the **-s**, all these plural nouns have an extra syllable. For example:

badge	bad-ge**s**
page	pa-ge**s**
sponge	spon-ge**s**

For nouns that end in **-ch**, you add **-es** to make them plural.

arch + **es** = arches

bench + **es** = benches

branch + **es** = branches

coach + **es** = coaches

peach + **es** = peaches

sketch + **es** = sketches

watch + **es** = watches

witch + **es** = witches

Word File

bunch	**bunches**
ditch	**ditches**
hutch	**hutches**
inch	**inches**
match	**matches**
torch	**torches**

For nouns that end in **-sh**, you add **-es** to make them plural.

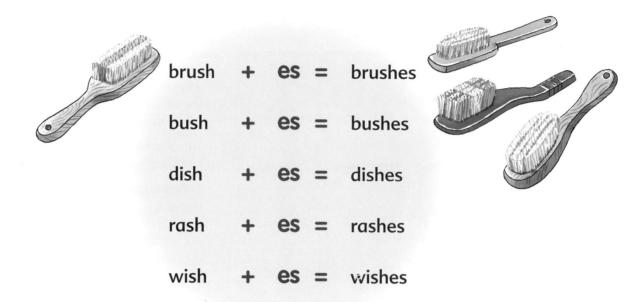

brush   **+**   **es** **=** brushes

bush   **+**   **es** **=** bushes

dish   **+**   **es** **=** dishes

rash   **+**   **es** **=** rashes

wish   **+**   **es** **=** wishes

For nouns that end in **-s** or **-ss**, you add **-es** to make them plural.

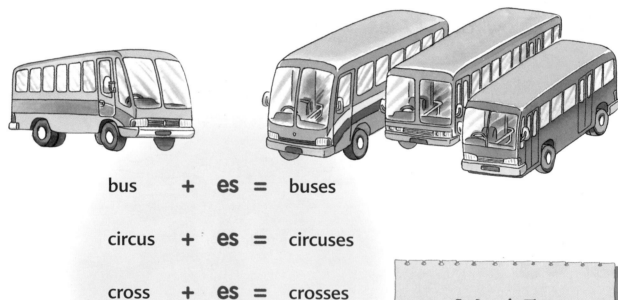

bus   **+**   **es** **=** buses

circus **+**   **es** **=** circuses

cross   **+**   **es** **=** crosses

dress   **+**   **es** **=** dresses

glass   **+**   **es** **=** glasses

Word File

abacus	**abacuses**
atlas	**atlases**
class	**classes**
lens	**lenses**
rhinoceros	**rhineroses**

For some nouns that end in **-x** and **-z**, you add **-es** to make them plural.

fox   **+**   **es**   **=**   foxes

box   **+**   **es**   **=**   boxes

fax   **+**   **es**   **=**   faxes

buzz   **+**   **es**   **=**   buzzes

waltz   **+**   **es**   **=**   waltzes

topaz   **+**   **es**   **=**   topazes

Did You Know

The words **quiz** and **fez** don't follow this rule. You double the **z** before adding **-es**:

fez   **fezzes**
quiz   **quizzes**

You add **-es** to some nouns that end in **-o** to make them plural.

flamingo	+	**es**	=	flamingoes
dingo	+	**es**	=	dingoes
hero	+	**es**	=	heroes
potato	+	**es**	=	potatoes
tomato	+	**es**	=	tomatoes
volcano	+	**es**	=	volcanoes

Did You Know

You have a choice of **s** or **es** with these nouns:

buffalo	**buffalos**	or	**buffaloes**
mango	**mangos**	or	**mangoes**
mosquito	**mosquitos**	or	**mosquitoes**
zero	**zeros**	or	**zeroes**

But for these nouns that end in **-o** or **-oo**, you just add **-s** to make them plural.

avocado + s = avocados

banjo	+	**s**	=	banjos
photo	+	**s**	=	photos
piano	+	**s**	=	pianos
rhino	+	**s**	=	rhinos
radio	+	**s**	=	radios
zoo	+	**s**	=	zoos

Word File

cello	**cellos**
cuckoo	**cuckoos**
kangaroo	**kangaroos**
kimono	**kimonos**
shampoo	**shampoos**

If the singular count nouns end in **-ce** or **-se,**
you just add **-s** to make them plural.

house + s = houses

face	+	s	=	faces
horse	+	s	=	horses
lace	+	s	=	laces
rose	+	s	=	roses
slice	+	s	=	slices
vase	+	s	=	vases
dance	+	s	=	dances
palace	+	s	=	palaces
race	+	s	=	races
space	+	s	=	spaces

Did You Know

These plural nouns all have one more syllable than their singular:

face	fa-ces
dance	dan-ces
horse	hor-ses
palace	pa-la-ces
rose	ro-ses
space	spa-ces

With some nouns that end in **-y**, you change the **y** to **i**, and add **-es** to make them plural.

cherry i + es = cherries

baby i	+	es	=	babies
fairy i	+	es	=	fairies
family i	+	es	=	families
library i	+	es	=	libraries
story i	+	es	=	stories
strawberry i	+	es	=	strawberries

But if there is a vowel before **y**, you just add **-s** to form the plural.

key + s = keys

day	+	s	=	days
donkey	+	s	=	donkeys
monkey	+	s	=	monkeys
runway	+	s	=	runways
tray	+	s	=	trays
trolley	+	s	=	trolleys
turkey	+	s	=	turkeys
valley	+	s	=	valleys
way	+	s	=	ways

With some nouns that end in **-f**, you change the **f** to **v**, and add **-es**.

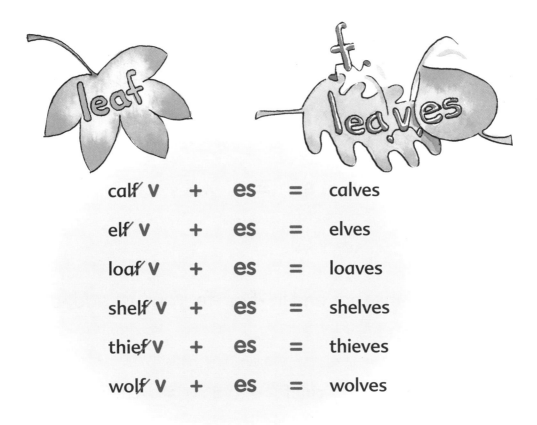

calf **v** + **es** = calves

elf **v** + **es** = elves

loaf **v** + **es** = loaves

shelf **v** + **es** = shelves

thief **v** + **es** = thieves

wolf **v** + **es** = wolves

With these words you have a choice of adding **-s** or **-es** to form the plural.

hoof   **hoofs** or **hooves**

scarf   **scarfs** or **scarves**

With some nouns that end in **-fe**, you change the **f** to **v**, and add **-s**.

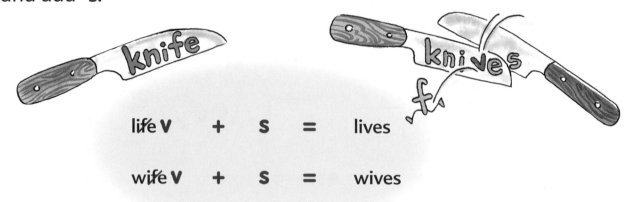

life **v** + **s** = lives

wife **v** + **s** = wives

But with some nouns that end in **-f** or **-fe**, you just add **-s** to form the plural.

chief + **s** = chiefs

cliff + **s** = cliffs

roof + **s** = roofs

safe + **s** = safes

+ **s**

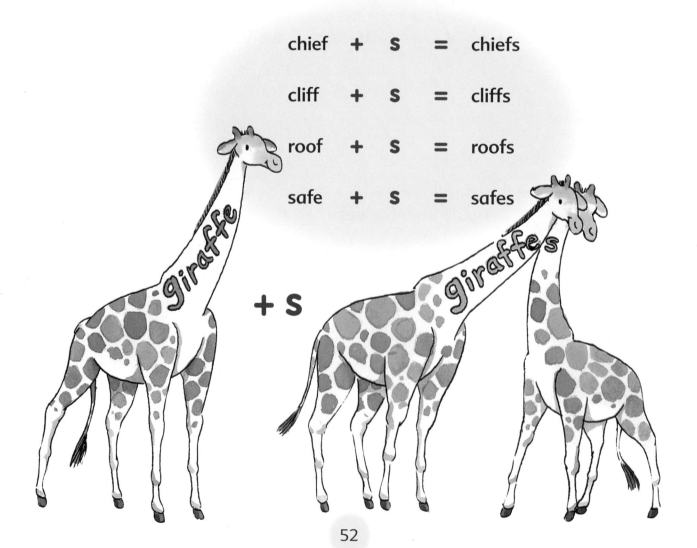

Some nouns have a plural form that doesn't end with **-s**.

mouse	—	mice
child	—	children
foot	—	feet
man	—	men
woman	—	women
tooth	—	teeth

These nouns have the same form for singular and plural.

aircraft	—	aircraft
deer	—	deer
fish	—	fish
sheep	—	sheep

Did You Know

The names of some animals have the same form for singular and plural:

carp	—	carp
cod	—	cod
salmon	—	salmon
trout	—	trout
reindeer	—	reindeer

Making Nouns

You can add **-er** or **-or** to some words to mean 'someone or something that does something'.

You can add **-er** to many verbs to form nouns.

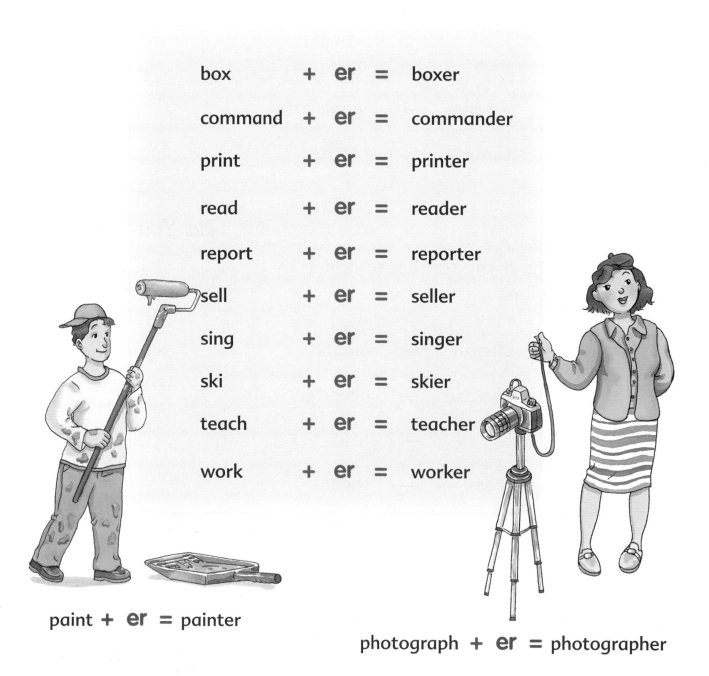

box	+ **er** =	boxer
command	+ **er** =	commander
print	+ **er** =	printer
read	+ **er** =	reader
report	+ **er** =	reporter
sell	+ **er** =	seller
sing	+ **er** =	singer
ski	+ **er** =	skier
teach	+ **er** =	teacher
work	+ **er** =	worker

paint **+ er** = painter

photograph **+ er** = photographer

But when the verbs end with a **silent e**, after one or more consonants, you just add **-r**.

bake **+ r =** baker

skate **+ r =** skater

compose **+ r =** composer

dance **+ r =** dancer

drive **+ r =** driver

explore **+ r =** explorer

invade **+ r =** invader

lose **+ r =** loser

make **+ r =** maker

manage **+ r =** manager

write **+ r =** writer

When verbs of one syllable end in a consonant, and have one vowel before the consonant, you double the consonant before adding **-er**.

swim + **m** + **er** = swimmer

drum + **m** + **er** = drummer

jog + **g** + **er** = jogger

rob + **b** + **er** = robber

run + **n** + **er** = runner

win + **n** + **er** = winner

With verbs of more than one syllable, you double the last consonant if the last syllable is stressed.

begin + **n** + **er** = beginner

kidnap + **p** + **er** = kidnapper

But with verbs that end in **-l**, you always double the l.

travel + **l** + **er** = traveller

control + **l** + **er** = controller

Did You Know

In American English, **traveller** is spelt **traveler**, with one l.

56

When a verb ends in **-y**, you change **y** to **i** before adding **-er** to from a noun.

carr~~y~~**i**   +   **er**   =   carrier

dr~~y~~ **i**   +   **er**   =   drier

fl~~y~~ **i**   +   **er**   =   flier

suppl~~y~~ **i** + **er**   =   supplier

cop~~y~~ **i** + **er** = copier

But if there is a vowel before the **y**, you keep the **y**, and add **-er**.

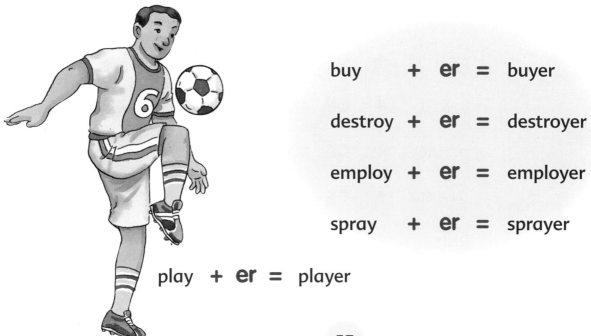

buy   + **er** = buyer

destroy + **er** = destroyer

employ + **er** = employer

spray   + **er** = sprayer

play + **er** = player

With some verbs, you have to add **-or** to form nouns meaning 'somebody or something that does something'.

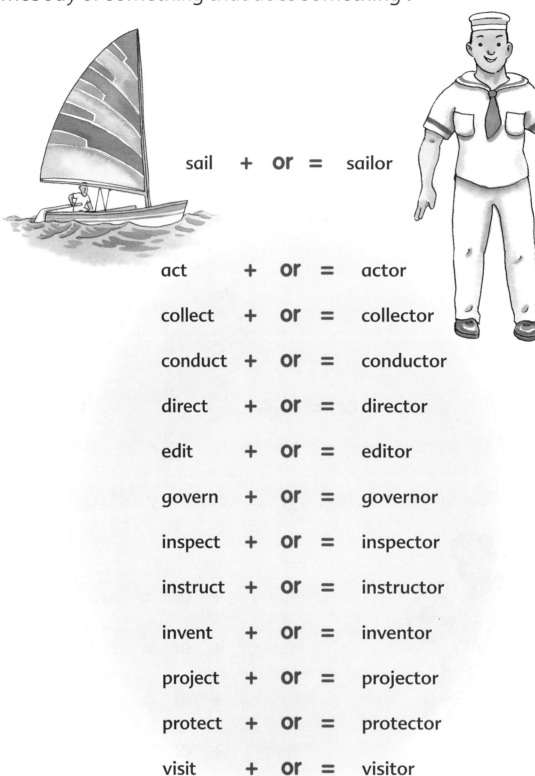

sail + **or** = sailor

act + **or** = actor

collect + **or** = collector

conduct + **or** = conductor

direct + **or** = director

edit + **or** = editor

govern + **or** = governor

inspect + **or** = inspector

instruct + **or** = instructor

invent + **or** = inventor

project + **or** = projector

protect + **or** = protector

visit + **or** = visitor

When the verbs end in **silent e**, you drop the **e** before adding **-or**.

illustrate + **or** = illustrator

create + **or** = creator

decorate + **or** = decorator

distribute + **or** = distributor

elevate + **or** = elevator

narrate + **or** = narrator

navigate + **or** = navigator

operate + **or** = operator

supervise + **or** = supervisor

You can add **-ness** to adjectives to make abstract nouns. Abstract nouns with **-ness** ending mean 'the state of being something'.

dark + **ness** = darkness

fair + **ness** = fairness

fit + **ness** = fitness

ill + **ness** = illness

kind + **ness** = kindness

thick + **ness** = thickness

sad + **ness** = sadness

When an adjective ends in **-y**, you change the **y** to **i**, and add **-ness** to form the nouns.

friendly**i** + **ness** = friendliness

lazy**i** + **ness** = laziness

lonely**i** + **ness** = loneliness

tidy**i** + **ness** = tidiness

ugly**i** + **ness** = ugliness

happy**i** + **ness** = happiness

60

5 Spelling Rules for Adjectives

You add **-ful** to nouns to change them to adjectives. These adjectives mean 'full of' or 'showing the quality of something'.

care + ful = careful
Be **careful** with that pile of plates!

colour + ful = colourful
Orchids are **colourful** flowers.

harm + ful = harmful
Some snakes can give you a **harmful** bite.

help + ful = helpful
A **helpful** lady took me across the road.

hope + ful = hopeful
Fido is looking at the sausages with a **hopeful** expression.

use + ful = useful
A penknife is a **useful** tool.

wonder + ful = wonderful
The fireworks were **wonderful**.

Did You Know

Words ending with a **silent e** keep their **e** before you add **-ful**. But there is an exception:

awe   **awful**

You drop the **e** from **awe** before adding **-ful**.

waste + ful = wasteful
It's **wasteful** to leave the tap running.

With nouns that end in **-y**, you change the **y** to **i**, and add **-ful**.

beaut~~y~~i + **ful** = beautiful
Our cat has two **beautiful** kittens.

merc~~y~~i + **ful** = merciful
A **merciful** person forgives others instead of punishing them.

pit~~y~~ i + **ful** = pitiful
That poor plant is in a **pitiful** state.

fanc~~y~~i + **ful** = fanciful
Dragons are **fanciful** creatures, not real ones.

But when there is a vowel before **-y**, you keep the **y**, and add **-ful**.

joy + **ful** = joyful   Christmas is a **joyful** time.
play + **ful** = playful   The puppies are having a **playful** fight.

With nouns that end in **-ll**, you drop one **l** before adding **-ful**.

ski~~l~~l + **ful** = skilful   The pilot made a **skilful** landing in a field.
wi~~l~~l + **ful** = wilful   **Wilful** children don't like obeying their parents or teachers.

You add **-less** to nouns to change them into adjectives.
Adjectives ending with **-less** generally mean 'without something'.

home + less = homeless
The earthquake left a lot of people **homeless.**

Did You Know

These adjectives are often opposites of the adjectives ending in **-ful**.

care	+ less	= careless	Look! You've made a **careless** mistake.
harm	+ less	= harmless	These insects don't sting; they're quite **harmless**.
leaf	+ less	= leafless	Snow was falling on the **leafless** trees.
seed	+ less	= seedless	These grapes are **seedless**.
spot	+ less	= spotless	A **spotless** floor is one that is very clean.

With nouns that end in **-y**, you change **y** to **i**, and add **-less**.

mercy i + less = merciless The plants withered in the **merciless** heat.

pity i + less = pitiless The slaves were often whipped by their **pitiless** master.

Did You Know

But you keep the **y** when there is a vowel before it, and add **-less**. For example:
money   **moneyless**

penny i + less = penniless
Jim had spent all his pocket money, so he was **penniless**.

Adjectives that end with **-able** and **-ible** mean 'that you can do something to'. You can add **-able** to many verbs to form adjectives.

break + able = breakable
Glass is a **breakable** material.

count + able = countable   Some nouns are **countable** and some are **uncountable**.

read + able = readable   The writing was **readable** only with a magnifying glass.

wash + able = washable   Is this dress **washable**, or should it be dry-cleaned?

These adjectives are spelt with **-ible** ending.

edible   Are these mushrooms **edible**?

legible   Your handwriting should be neat and **legible**.

visible   Land was **visible** on the horizon.

Here are more adjectives that end with **-able** or **-ible**.

comfortable   Are you **comfortable** sitting on the floor?

responsible   Who is **responsible** for watering the flowers this week?

suitable   We're trying to think of a **suitable** name for our puppy.

terrible   It would be **terrible** if I failed my exam.

horrible
I think there's a **horrible** monster under my bed.

With some verbs ending in **-e**, you drop the **e** before adding **-able**.

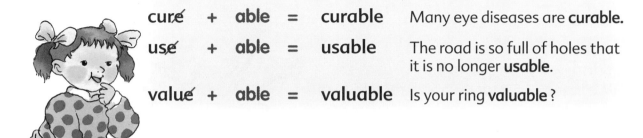

curé	+	**able**	=	curable	Many eye diseases are **curable**.
usé	+	**able**	=	usable	The road is so full of holes that it is no longer **usable**.
valué	+	**able**	=	valuable	Is your ring **valuable**?

adoré + **able** = adorable
What an **adorable** little baby!

With other verbs ending in **-e**, you keep the **e** and add **-able**.

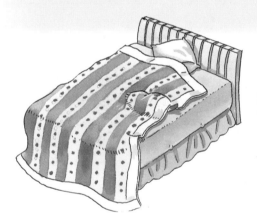

change + **able** = changeable
The weather has been very **changeable** lately.

notice + **able** = noticeable
There was a **noticeable** lump in the bed.

These adjectives can be spelt with or without **e** before **-able**.

love   loveable or lovable
Would a crocodile be a **loveable** (or **lovable**) pet?

move   moveable or movable
Chinese New Year is a **moveable** (or **movable**) feast.

like   likeable or likable
Kenneth is a **likeable** (or **likable**) boy.

Adjectives that end with **-y** generally mean 'having a lot of something'. You can add **y** to many nouns to form adjectives.

sand + y = sandy
We found a nice **sandy** beach for our swim.

cloud	+	**y**	=	**cloudy**

In Singapore the weather is often **cloudy** and wet.

dirt + **y** = **dirty** — Take off your **dirty** shoes before coming indoors.

dust + **y** = **dusty** — The furniture looks a bit **dusty**.

health + **y** = **healthy** — Enjoy life while you're young and **healthy**.

rain + **y** = **rainy** — We had a lot of **rainy** weather when we were in Britain.

rust + **y** = **rusty** — What makes iron go **rusty**?

storm + **y** = **stormy** — **Stormy** weather has been forecast for the weekend.

Word File

gloom	**gloomy**
hair	**hairy**
luck	**lucky**
mess	**messy**
milk	**milky**
mood	**moody**
oil	**oily**
snow	**snowy**

wind + y = windy
It often gets **windy** in the afternoons here.

With nouns that end with a **silent e**, you drop the **e**, and add **-y**.

bubble + y = bubbly
Do you like **bubbly** drinks such as Coke?

wave + y = wavy
Can you draw a **wavy** line?

ease + y =	**easy**	It isn't **easy** to walk on your hands.
haze + y =	**hazy**	When it's misty on a hot sunny day, you say it's **hazy**.
juice + y =	**juicy**	Dessert was a plate of **juicy** melons and papayas.
noise + y =	**noisy**	The playground is full of **noisy** children.
rose + y =	**rosy**	Taking exercise gives you **rosy** cheeks.
smoke + y =	**smoky**	Cigarettes make the room **smoky**.
stone + y =	**stony**	I don't like walking barefoot on a **stony** beach.
taste + y =	**tasty**	The meal started with some hot **tasty** soup.

With nouns that have only one vowel and end with a consonant, you double the consonant before adding **-y**.

fur + r + y = **furry**
This coat has a **furry** collar and cuffs.

fog + g + y = **foggy**   It's too **foggy** to see the island today.

fun + n + y = **funny**   Sally has made a **funny** monkey mask.

mud + d + y = **muddy**   Wipe your **muddy** feet before you come inside.

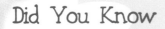

skin + n + y = **skinny**   A **skinny** person is someone who is very thin.

star + r + y = **starry**   The sky is **starry** when there are no clouds.

sun + n + y = **sunny**   The day of the picnic dawned bright and **sunny**.

wit + t + y = **witty**   A **witty** person says funny things and makes you laugh.

bag + g + y = **baggy**
Sam is wearing a pair of very **baggy** jeans.

6 Spelling Rules for Adverbs

Many adverbs are spelt with an **-ly** at the end.
You form them by adding **-ly** to adjectives.

sad + **ly** = sadly
Granny waved goodbye **sadly** as we left.

brave	**+**	**ly**	**= bravely**	Anna **bravely** dived off the top diving board.
free	**+**	**ly**	**= freely**	The animals wander about **freely** in the night safari.
foolish	**+**	**ly**	**= foolishly**	I **foolishly** forgot to bring my key with me.
kind	**+**	**ly**	**= kindly**	The waitress **kindly** cleaned up the spilt juice.
neat	**+**	**ly**	**= neatly**	You have written your exercise very **neatly**.
nice	**+**	**ly**	**= nicely**	The table will fit **nicely** into that space.
quick	**+**	**ly**	**= quickly**	Help me **quickly**, before I drop these parcels.
quiet	**+**	**ly**	**= quietly**	The baby is asleep, so speak **quietly**.
safe	**+**	**ly**	**= safely**	Do you know how to cross the road **safely**?
slow	**+**	**ly**	**= slowly**	Walk **slowly**; I can't keep up.
sure	**+**	**ly**	**= surely**	**Surely** you can do that sum?

If the adjectives end in **-y**, you have to change the **y** to **i** before adding **-ly**.

angry̶ i + ly = angrily
The policeman spoke **angrily** to the driver.

tidy̶ i + ly = tidily
We put the books **tidily** back on the shelves.

busy̶ i	**+**	**ly**	**=**	**busily**	People are shopping **busily** in the supermarket.
easy̶ i	**+**	**ly**	**=**	**easily**	You can **easily** see the Grand Hotel from here.
greedy̶ i	**+**	**ly**	**=**	**greedily**	I **greedily** ate two whole packets of chips.
hasty̶ i	**+**	**ly**	**=**	**hastily**	Mr Kumar **hastily** switched off his mobile phone.
heavy̶ i	**+**	**ly**	**=**	**heavily**	The baby walked two steps, then fell **heavily** down on his bottom.
lazy̶ i	**+**	**ly**	**=**	**lazily**	We sunbathed **lazily** beside the swimming pool all morning.
lucky̶ i	**+**	**ly**	**=**	**luckily**	**Luckily** the train left late, so I caught it.
merry̶ i	**+**	**ly**	**=**	**merrily**	The bells are ringing **merrily** to celebrate Christmas.
ready̶ i	**+**	**ly**	**=**	**readily**	The children **readily** stood up to greet Miss Lee.

When you add **-ly** to adjectives that end in **-ful**, remember that you get **-ll-**.

tearful + ly = tearfully
'My watch is broken,' said David **tearfully**.

beautiful + ly = beautifully   You have decorated the Christmas tree **beautifully**.

careful + ly = carefully   Carry these dishes **carefully**.

cheerful + ly = cheerfully   Sue sings **cheerfully** as she cleans the house.

faithful + ly = faithfully   The dog **faithfully** followed his master everywhere.

graceful + ly = gracefully   Point your toe **gracefully**.

hopeful + ly = hopefully   **Hopefully**, I'll be chosen for the football team.

joyful + ly = joyfully   My puppy welcomed me **joyfully** when I got home.

painful + ly = painfully   The old lady hobbled **painfully** along the street.

peaceful + ly = peacefully   It is night and everybody is sleeping **peacefully**.

pitiful + ly = pitifully   The cattle are **pitifully** thin.

playful + ly = playfully   My puppy bit me **playfully** on the ankle.

skilful + ly = skilfully   Ben **skilfully** drew a circle with his pencil.

If the adjectives end in **-le**, you just change the **e** to **y** to form adverbs.

single + y = singly
Come forward **singly** as I read out your name.

comfortable	+ y =	comfortably	Are you sitting **comfortably**?
double	+ y =	doubly	It was **doubly** exciting to fly to Britain and to see Granny again.
gentle	+ y =	gently	Handle the computer **gently**.
idle	+ y =	idly	You can dry the dishes instead of standing there **idly**.
legible	+ y =	legibly	Always write neatly and **legibly**.
possible	+ y =	possibly	I can't **possibly** climb up that rock.
simple	+ y =	simply	Miss Lee is good at explaining things **simply** to us.
terrible	+ y =	terribly	These sums are **terribly** difficult.

Spelling Rules for Verbs

The Third Person Singular

You put **-s** at the end of most verbs when you use them with the pronouns **he**, **she** and **it**, and with **singular nouns**. The **-s** form of the verbs is known as the **third person singular**.

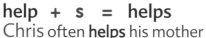

help + s = helps
Chris often **helps** his mother with the housework.

travel + s = travels
Mum is a school inspector, so she **travels** a lot.

bend + s = bends
This branch is not strong. It **bends** easily.

bark	+ s	=	**barks**	Our dog usually **barks** at strangers.
build	+ s	=	**builds**	The male bird **builds** a nest for the female bird and her babies.
draw	+ s	=	**draws**	Every morning the servant **draws** water from the well.
drink	+ s	=	**drinks**	Dad **drinks** tea with his colleagues every afternoon.
hide	+ s	=	**hides**	In this game, one girl **hides**, and the others look for her.
open	+ s	=	**opens**	The pharmacy **opens** at 8.30 in the morning.
play	+ s	=	**plays**	Our team **plays** Monty School this Saturday.

You add **-es** instead of **-s** to verbs that end in **-sh** and **-ss**, to form the third person singular.

pass + es = passes
The bus **passes** our house every morning at eight o'clock.

brush + es = brushes
Paul always **brushes** his teeth after breakfast.

crash + **es** = **crashes**   Each wave makes a huge noise as it **crashes** into the rocks.

finish + **es** = **finishes**   Joan usually **finishes** her homework by six o'clock.

push + **es** = **pushes**   The assistant **pushes** all the supermarket trolleys back into the store.

vanish + **es** = **vanishes**   When dawn comes the moon **vanishes**.

wash + **es** = **washes**   Mandy **washes** her hair everyday in the shower.

cross + **es** = **crosses**
Sue always looks both ways before
she **crosses** over.

dress + **es** = **dresses**   Miss Lee **dresses** very smartly.

hiss + **es** = **hisses**   The snake **hisses** at its prey.

miss + **es** = **misses**   Dave **misses** his mother when she's away
on business.

polish + es = polishes
Dad **polishes** his shoes till
they shine.

Word File

blush	**blushes**
clash	**clashes**
discuss	**discusses**
dismiss	**dismisses**
fish	**fishes**
flush	**flushes**
guess	**guesses**
kiss	**kisses**
possess	**possesses**
press	**presses**
punish	**punishes**
rush	**rushes**
wish	**wishes**

You add **-es** instead of **-s** to verbs that end in **-ch** to form the third person singular.

fetch + es = fetches
Dad **fetches** the children from their swimming class on a Thursday.

catch	+ es	=	catches	Each person **catches** the ball and throws it to the next person.
itch	+ es	=	itches	Chickenpox causes a rash which **itches** and **itches**.
march	+ es	=	marches	Our class **marches** smartly into Assembly every morning.
perch	+ es	=	perches	In the evenings a pigeon comes and **perches** on my window sill.

hatch + es = hatches
The chick breaks through the shell
as it **hatches** out.

preach + es = preaches   The pastor **preaches** in church every Sunday.

punch + es = punches   Fred sometimes **punches** his brother when no-one is looking.

snatch + es = snatches   The wind is sometimes so strong that it **snatches** your hat off.

stitch + es = stitches   Maggie cuts out the pattern and **stitches** the pieces together.

watch + es = watches
Our cat **watches** the birds from the
window, longing to chase them.

Word File

attach	**attaches**
launch	**launches**
match	**matches**
pinch	**pinches**
reach	**reaches**
search	**searches**
stretch	**stretches**
teach	**teaches**
touch	**touches**

You add **-es** to verbs that end in **-o**, **-x** and **-z** to form the third person singular.

do + es = does
Sue **does** her exercises in front of the mirror every morning.

echo + es = echoes   Your voice **echoes** round the cave when you shout.

fax + es = faxes   Mum **faxes** messages to her friends from her computer.

fizz + es = fizzes   The lemonade **fizzes** when you unscrew the bottle top.

go + es = goes   Tom lives next door. He **goes** to Bedok Primary School.

mix + es = mixes   The machine **mixes** the fruit with the ice cream.

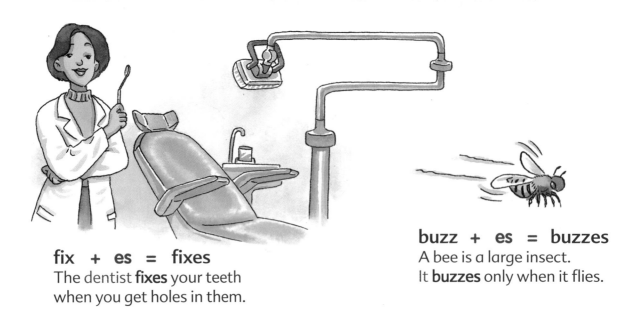

fix + es = fixes
The dentist **fixes** your teeth when you get holes in them.

buzz + es = buzzes
A bee is a large insect. It **buzzes** only when it flies.

With verbs that end in **-y** and have a consonant before the **y**, you change **y** to **i**, and add **-es** to form the third person singular.

bur~~y~~i + es = buries
Our dog **buries** his bones in the garden.

appl~~y~~i + es = applies   The rule **applies** to all children in the primary schools.

cop~~y~~i + es = copies   Our parrot **copies** some of the things we say.

cr~~y~~i + es = cries   The baby usually **cries** when she's hungry.

carr~~y~~i + es = carries
I like my big brother. He often **carries** me on his shoulders.

Here are more verbs that end in **y**. You change the **y** to **i** before adding **-es** to form the third person singular.

fly̸i + es = flies
This plane **flies** to and from Britain every day.

dry̸i + es = dries   Sally **dries** the dishes after Mum has washed them.

study̸i + es = studies   A university student **studies** the subjects that

he or she likes best.

try̸i + es = tries   The baby bird keeps falling down when it first

tries to fly.

marry̸i + es = marries
A girl is called a bride when
she **marries.**

But you don't drop the **y** if there is a vowel **a, e, o** or **u** before it. You just add **-s** after the **y**.

pay + s = pays
Each customer **pays** for their goods at the checkout.

say + s = says
This notice **says** 'Keep left'.

enjoy + s = enjoys
A puppy **enjoys** being patted and played with.

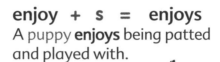

annoy	+	**s**	=	**annoys**	It **annoys** mum when we mess up the kitchen.
buy	+	**s**	=	**buys**	Susan sometimes **buys** clothes for herself.
lay	+	**s**	=	**lays**	George **lays** the table every evening for dinner.
obey	+	**s**	=	**obeys**	A careful driver always **obeys** road signs.
play	+	**s**	=	**plays**	My sister **plays** the guitar, the piano and the trumpet.
stay	+	**s**	=	**stays**	Mike often **stays** with his aunt in Penang.

The Present Participle

The **-ing** form is called the **present participle** or **gerund**. You use it to make the present continuous tense or past continuous tense. With most verbs, you just add **-ing** to their base form.

fish + ing = fishing

read + ing = reading

drink + ing = drinking

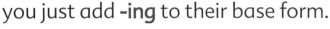

Did You Know

You use the **present continuous tense** to talk about actions in the present, or things that are going on now.

You use the **past continuous tense** to talk about actions that were going on, or happening at a certain moment in the past.

eat	+	ing	=	eating

eat + ing = eating — We are **eating** at a new restaurant today.

fly + ing = flying — This plane is **flying** to Bangkok.

play + ing = playing — Some kids are **playing** football in the field.

shoot + ing = shooting — Dave is **shooting** at goal.

sing + ing = singing — I don't think you were **singing** in tune.

sleep + ing = sleeping — Everyone was **sleeping** peacefully when Santa Claus arrived.

82

With verbs that end with an **-e**, you usually have to drop the **e** before you add **-ing**.

shake + **ing** = **shaking**
We were all **shaking** with laughter.

chase + **ing** = **chasing**
The dog was **chasing** the cat around the garden.

ride	+	**ing**	=	**riding**	Jill is **riding** her pony round the field.
rise	+	**ing**	=	**rising**	The sun was just **rising** when I looked out of the window.
share	+	**ing**	=	**sharing**	I'm **sharing** these sweets with my friends.
take	+	**ing**	=	**taking**	Mum is **taking** Jimmy to nursery school.
wave	+	**ing**	=	**waving**	Granny is **waving** goodbye from the door.

drive + **ing** = **driving**
Dad is **driving** the car through the gates.

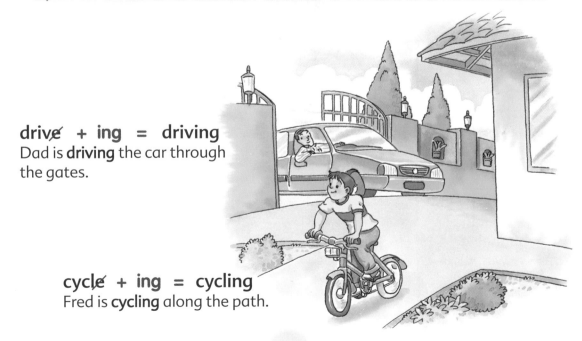

cycle + **ing** = **cycling**
Fred is **cycling** along the path.

With verbs that have only one short vowel, and end with a consonant, you have to double the last consonant before adding **-ing**.

fan + n + ing = fanning
Helen is **fanning** herself because she is too hot.

jog + g + ing = jogging
People are **jogging** around the park.

clap + p + ing = clapping   The children are **clapping** in time with the piano.

hop + p + ing = hopping   A little bird is **hopping** along the path.

hug + g + ing = hugging   Carol is **hugging** her puppy.

rub + b + ing = rubbing   We were all **rubbing** sun cream over ourselves.

stop + p + ing = stopping   I was just **stopping** to look in this shop window.

pat + t + ing = patting
I'm patting my dog's head.

Word File

ban	**banning**
beg	**begging**
chat	**chatting**
drop	**dropping**
hum	**humming**
nod	**nodding**
plan	**planning**
rob	**robbing**
swim	**swimming**
tap	**tapping**
wag	**wagging**

Did You Know

These verbs have only one syllable. They end with consonants such as **b, d, g, m, n, p** or **t**.

With verbs of more than one syllable that end with the consonant **l**, and with one vowel before the **l**, you always double the **l** before adding **-ing**.

control + l + ing = controlling
A policeman is **controlling** the traffic at the crossing.

cancel + l + ing = cancelling   The Prime Minister is ill and he is **cancelling** all his appointments.

label + l + ing = labelling   Mum is **labelling** her luggage.

patrol + l + ing = patrolling   A police car is **patrolling** the streets.

pedal + l + ing = pedalling   Alice is **pedalling** as fast as she can.

signal + l + ing = signalling   The officer is **signalling** to us to stop.

travel + l + ing = travelling
We were **travelling** in Europe when our car broke down.

Did You Know

In American English you do not double the **l** before adding **-ing**:

cancel	**canceling**
label	**labeling**
pedal	**pedaling**
signal	**signaling**
travel	**traveling**

You just add **-ing** to verbs that end in **-ee**, **-oe** or **-ye**.

flee + ing = fleeing
We were all **fleeing** from the angry wasps.

agree + ing = agreeing   You nod your head to show you are **agreeing** with somebody.

free + ing = freeing   The jailor is **freeing** all the prisoners.

see + ing = seeing   Am I **seeing** a ghost?

canoe + ing = canoeing
We spent a week **canoeing** along the river.

dye + ing = dyeing   Sally is **dyeing** all her clothes purple.

eye + ing = eyeing   The dog must be hungry. It is **eyeing** the piece of meat.

hoe + ing = hoeing   Mary is **hoeing** the vegetable patch.

tiptoe + ing = tiptoeing   We are **tiptoeing** out of the baby's nursery.

With verbs ending in **-ie**, you change **ie** to **y** before adding **-ing**.

lie y + ing = lying
Do you like **lying** in the sun?

tie y + ing = tying
Dad was **tying** his shoes when a shoelace broke.

die y + ing = dying
I think these flowers are **dying**.

The Past Participle

You usually add **-ed** to the base form of verbs to make the simple past tense and past participle.

boil + ed = boiled
We **boiled** the dumplings in a big pot.

jump + ed = jumped
We **jumped** into the swimming pool one by one.

cross + ed = crossed
Dave **crossed** the road using the pedestrain crossing.

bark	+ **ed** =	barked	The dog **barked** at the sound of the doorbell.
check	+ **ed** =	checked	Have you **checked** all your sums?
clean	+ **ed** =	cleaned	Yesterday I **cleaned** the rabbit's hutch.
comb	+ **ed** =	combed	You haven't **combed** your hair this morning.
cook	+ **ed** =	cooked	Mum has **cooked** a special meal for my birthday.
discover	+ **ed** =	discovered	I've **discovered** a new computer game.
help	+ **ed** =	helped	Helen **helped** Mum to make the beds.

You just add **-d** to most verbs that end with an **-e** to form the simple past tense.

queue + d = queued
We **queued** for two hours for tickets for the match.

change	+	**d**	=	**changed**	George **changed** into his jeans and tee-shirt.
chase	+	**d**	=	**chased**	The cat **chased** the mouse into its hole.
close	+	**d**	=	**closed**	I **closed** the door very quietly.

Word File

blame	**blamed**	gaze	**gazed**
create	**created**	grade	**graded**
cycle	**cycled**	hope	**hoped**
dance	**danced**	like	**liked**
dive	**dived**	paddle	**paddled**
divide	**divided**	vote	**voted**

Here are more verbs that end in **-e**. With these verbs you just add **-d** to form the simple past tense.

paste + d = pasted
I've **pasted** all these pictures into my scrapbook.

bake + d = baked
Mike has **baked** a butter cake.

guide	+ **d**	=	**guided**	A friend of Dad's **guided** us round London.
invite	+ **d**	=	**invited**	Kenneth has **invited** me to his party.
live	+ **d**	=	**lived**	Mum **lived** on a farm when she was a little girl.
love	+ **d**	=	**loved**	We **loved** watching the chimpanzees when we were at the zoo.

Did You Know?

If the verb ends with the sound **d** or **t**, the simple past tense has an extra syllable. Here are some examples:

created	crea-ted	**graded**	gra-ded
dated	da-ted	**guided**	gui-ded
divided	di-vi-ded	**invited**	in-vi-ted
faded	fa-ded	**recited**	re-ci-ted

With verbs that have one vowel and end with a consonant, you have to double the last consonant before adding **-ed** to form the simple past tense.

pin + n + ed = pinned
Sally **pinned** the flower to her dress.

grab + b + ed = grabbed
I **grabbed** an orange to take with me for lunch.

clap	+ **p**	+ **ed**	=	**clapped**	The children **clapped** along with the music.
drop	+ **p**	+ **ed**	=	**dropped**	I've **dropped** my key somewhere.
fan	+ **n**	+ **ed**	=	**fanned**	Dad **fanned** himself with his newspaper.
pat	+ **t**	+ **ed**	=	**patted**	The trainer **patted** the horse's nose.
skid	+ **d**	+ **ed**	=	**skidded**	I **skidded** on the ice and fell down.
stop	+ **p**	+ **ed**	=	**stopped**	We **stopped** at the traffic lights.

Did You Know

These verbs have only one syllable. If the verbs end with the sound *d* or *t*, you get the extra syllable in the simple past tense. Here are some examples:

dotted	dot-ted
fitted	fit-ted
knitted	knit-ted
nodded	nod-ded
patted	pat-ted
skidded	skid-ded
spotted	spot-ted

slam + m + ed = slammed
George **slammed** the door angrily.

With verbs that end in **-y**, you change the **y** to **i**, and add **-ed** to form the simple past tense.

bur~~y~~i + ed = buried
We **buried** Dad up to his neck in the sand.

cr~~y~~i + ed = cried   The baby **cried** for a while before falling asleep.

dr~~y~~i + ed = dried   I **dried** my hair with the hairdryer.

fr~~y~~i + ed = fried   We **fried** the mushrooms and beansprouts in the wok.

repl~~y~~i + ed = replied   Have you **replied** to Kenneth's invitation?

tid~~y~~i + ed = tidied   If you have **tidied** your desks you may go home.

tr~~y~~i + ed = tried   I've never **tried** skating before.

sp~~y~~i + ed = spied
We **spied** a bird sitting on the top branch of the tree.

carr~~y~~i + ed = carried
Helen **carried** the tray of drinks out into the garden.

hurr~~y~~i + ed = hurried
I **hurried** along the pavement to catch the bus.

Word File

dirty	**dirtied**
empty	**emptied**
envy	**envied**
pity	**pitied**
worry	**worried**

91

If a verb has a vowel before the **y**, you just add **-ed** to form the simple past tense.

enjoy + ed = enjoyed
We all **enjoyed** the circus.

sway + ed = swayed
The trees **swayed** to and fro in the wind.

Did You Know

These verbs don't follow this rule.

lay	laid
pay	paid
say	said

They are called **irregular verbs**.

obey	+	**ed**	=	**obeyed**	Miss Lee's pupils always **obeyed** her instructions.
play	+	**ed**	=	**played**	I **played** chess with Dad all evening.
pray	+	**ed**	=	**prayed**	The people **prayed** to the gods for rain.
prey	+	**ed**	=	**preyed**	Owls have always **preyed** on small animals such as mice.

destroy + ed = destroyed
The storm has **destroyed** the crops.

Word File

annoy	**annoyed**
betray	**betrayed**
employ	**employed**
okay	**okayed**
stay	**stayed**

If the verbs end in the consonant **l**, and there is a single vowel before it, you always double the **l** before adding **-ed**.

patrol + l + ed = patrolled
Police cars **patrolled** the streets every night.

pedal + l + ed = pedalled
Katie **pedalled** her tricycle round the garden.

cancel + l + ed = cancelled   The match has been **cancelled**.

control + l + ed = controlled   The crossing is **controlled** by traffic lights.

label + l + ed = labelled   Have you **labelled** all your suitcases?

travel + l + ed = travelled   My uncle has **travelled** all over the world.

Did You Know

This rule is the same as the rule for **-ing**.

In American English you do not double the **l** before adding **-ed**. For example:

cancel	**canceled**
label	**labeled**
pedal	**pedaled**
signal	**signaled**
travel	**traveled**

signal + l + ed = signalled
Dad **signalled** that he was turning left.

Many verbs in English do not add **-ed** to form the simple past tense and past participle. These verbs are called **irregular verbs**.

Here are some irregular verbs.

Base Form	Simple Past	Past Participle
blow	blew	blown
break	broke	broken
build	built	built
cut	cut	cut
dig	dug	dug
draw	drew	drawn
drink	drank	drunk
drive	drove	driven
eat	ate	eaten
give	gave	given
hide	hid	hidden
hurt	hurt	hurt
lose	lost	lost
ring	rang	rung
shut	shut	shut
teach	taught	taught

My Own Spelling File